HIDE and SEEK
MOON
The Moon Phases

BY ROBIN KOONTZ

ILLUSTRATED BY
CHRIS DAVIDSON

Consultant: James Pierce, PhD
Professor of Astronomy
Minnesota State University, Mankato
Mankato, Minnesota

CAPSTONE PRESS
a capstone imprint

First Graphics are published by Capstone Press,
1710 Roe Crest Drive, North Mankato, Minnesota 56003.
www.capstonepub.com

Books published by Capstone Press are manufactured with paper
containing at least 10 percent post-consumer waste.

Library of Congress Cataloging-in-Publication Data
Koontz, Robin Michal.
  Hide and seek moon : the moon phases / by Robin Koontz ; illustrated by
Chris Davidson.
      p. cm.—(First graphics. nature cycles)
  Summary: "In graphic novel format, text and illustrations describe the eight
phases of the moon"—Provided by publisher.
  Includes bibliographical references and index.
  ISBN 978-1-4296-5365-7 (library binding)
  ISBN 978-1-4296-6229-1 (paperback)
  1. Moon—Phases—Juvenile literature. 2. Moon—Comic books, strips, etc.—
Juvenile literature. I. Davidson, Chris, 1974– ill. II. Title.
  QB588.K66 2011
  523.3′2—dc22   2010030092

Editor: **Christopher L. Harbo**
Designer: **Lori Bye**
Art Director: **Nathan Gassman**
Production Specialist: **Eric Manske**

Printed in the United States of America in Stevens Point, Wisconsin.
092011   006391R

Table of Contents

Moon Mystery

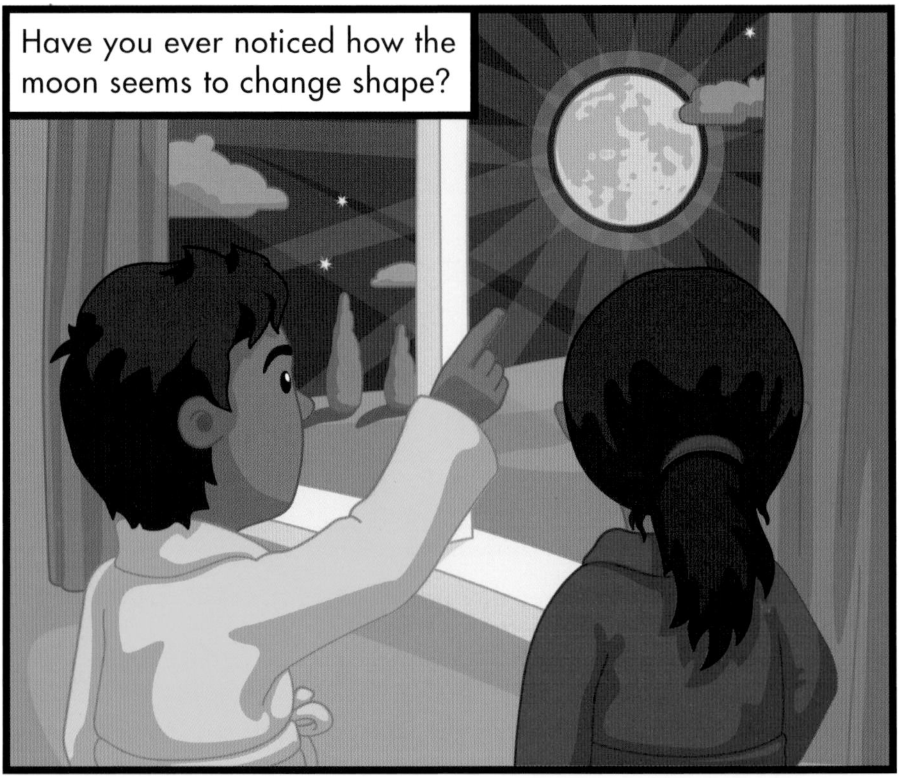
Have you ever noticed how the moon seems to change shape?

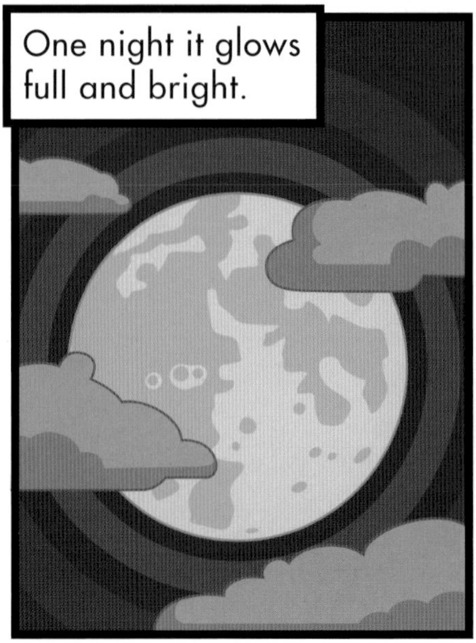
One night it glows full and bright.

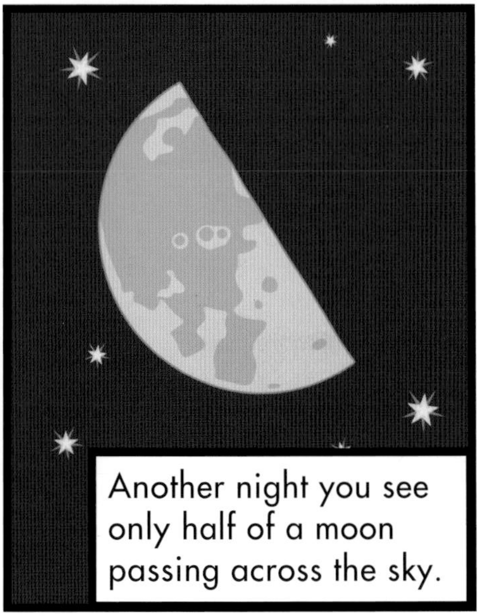
Another night you see only half of a moon passing across the sky.

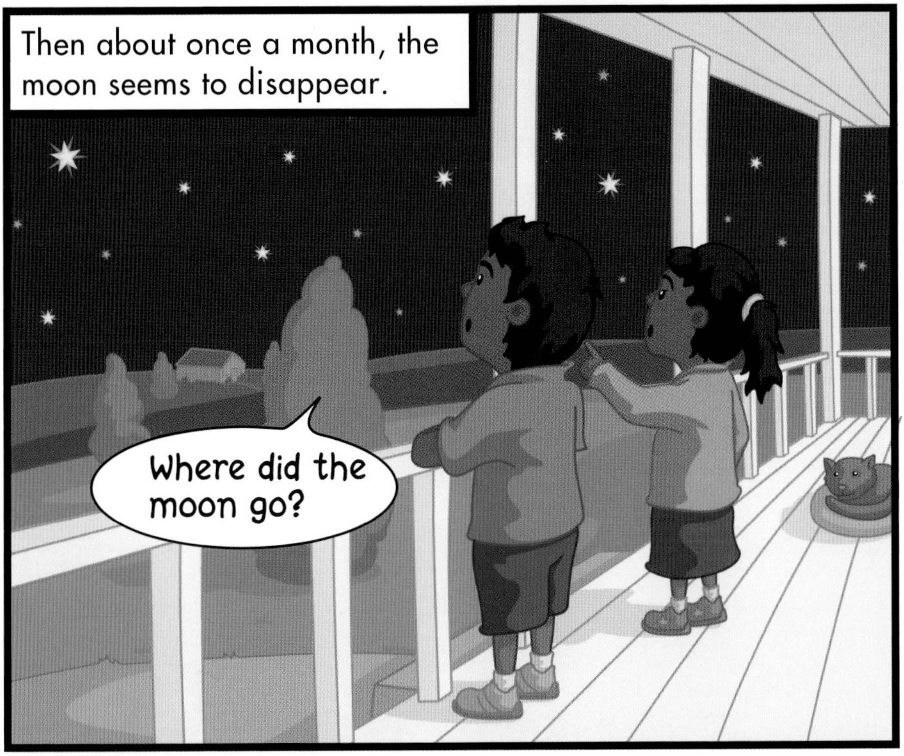
Then about once a month, the moon seems to disappear.
Where did the moon go?

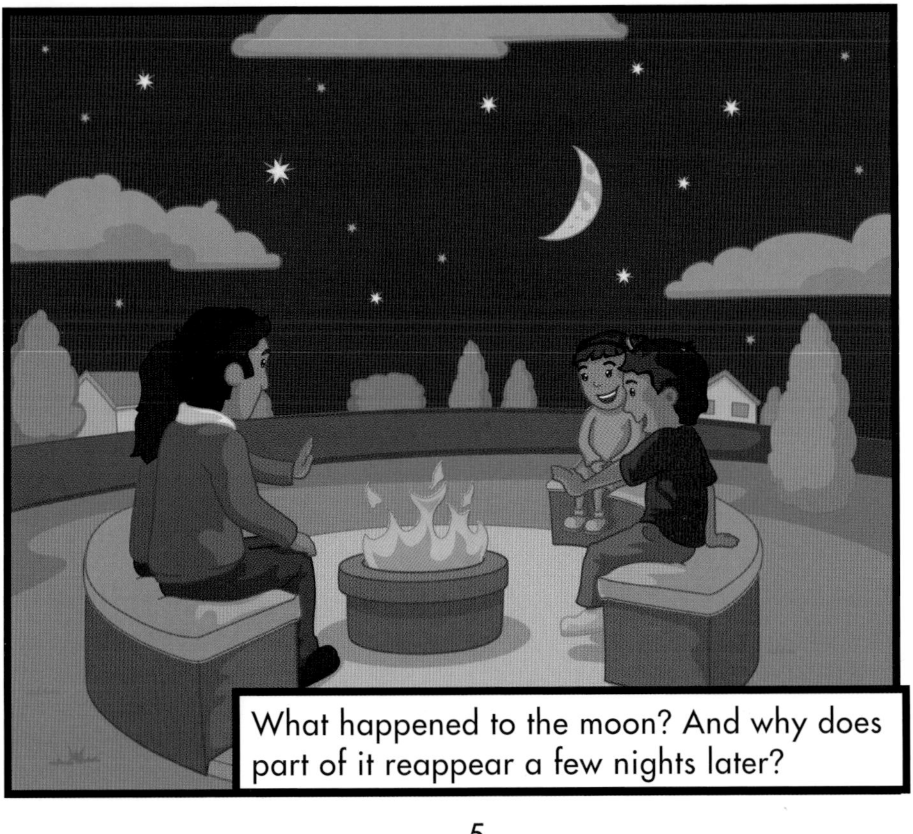
What happened to the moon? And why does part of it reappear a few nights later?

The Secret of Moonlight

Sunlight is the key to how the moon looks each night. Unlike a star, the moon does not create light. Instead, it reflects sunlight.

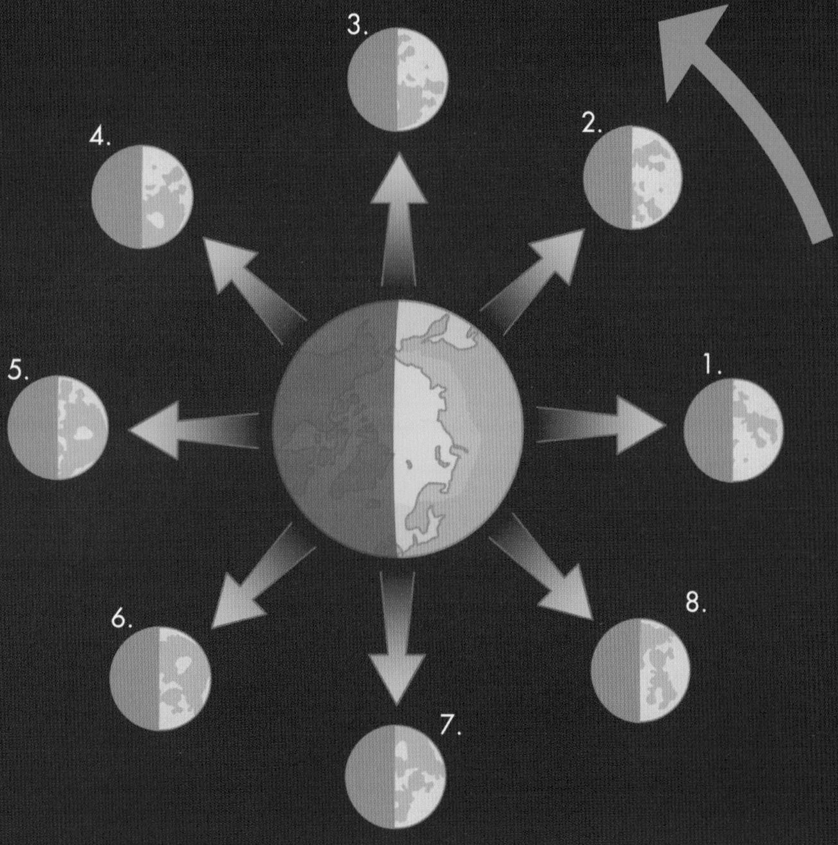

3.

4.

2.

5.

1.

6.

8.

7.

The moon circles Earth. As it does, only one side of the moon's surface faces us.

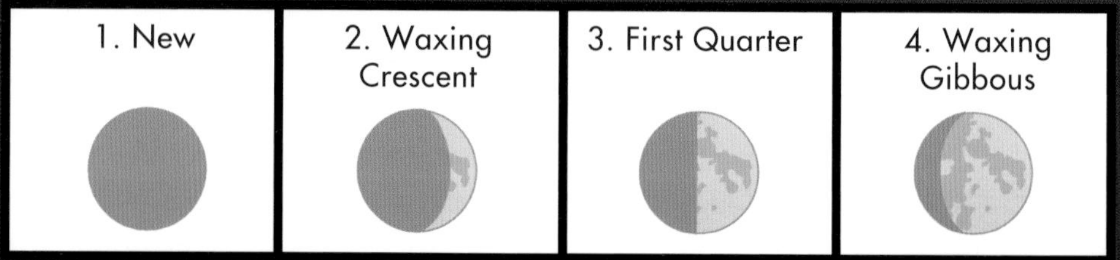

1. New	2. Waxing Crescent	3. First Quarter	4. Waxing Gibbous

Stages show moon's view from Earth.

Every night the amount of the moon's surface that reflects sunlight changes. That's why the moon looks different each night.

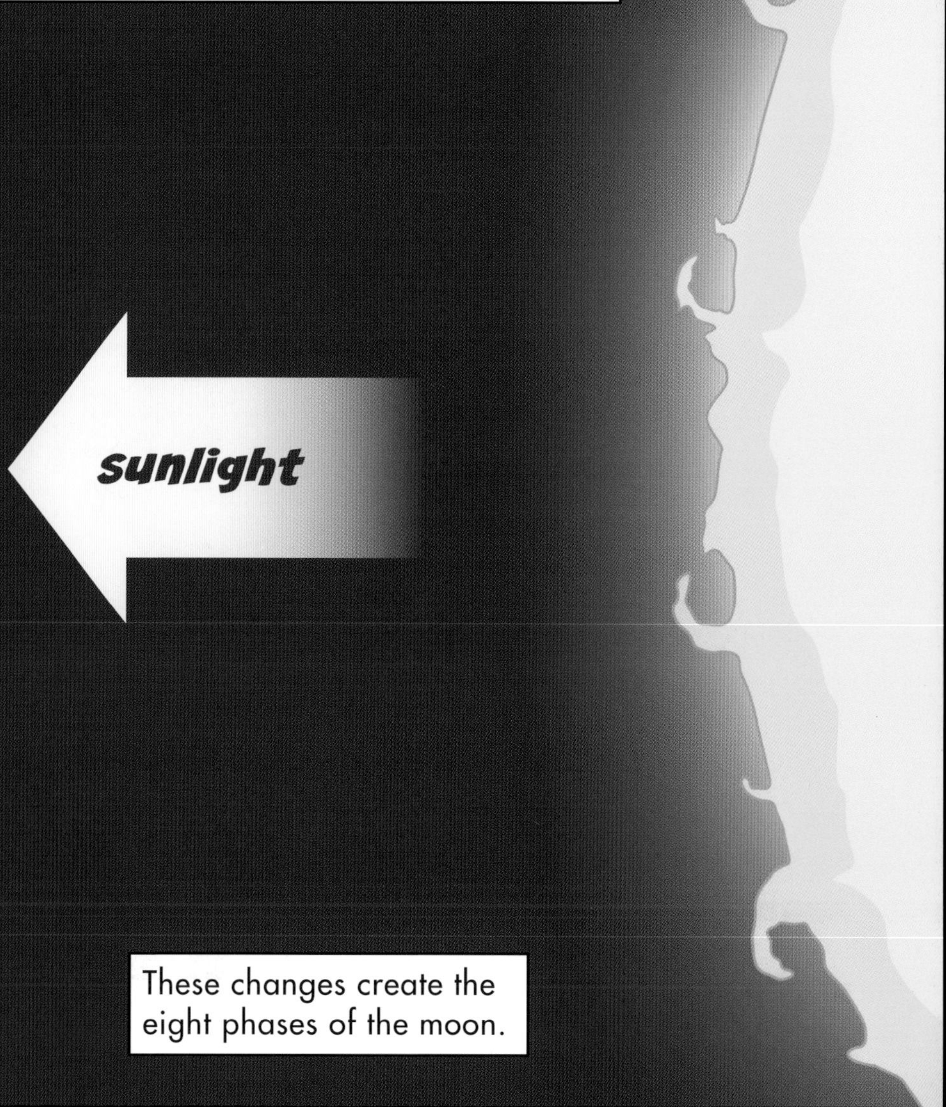

sunlight

These changes create the eight phases of the moon.

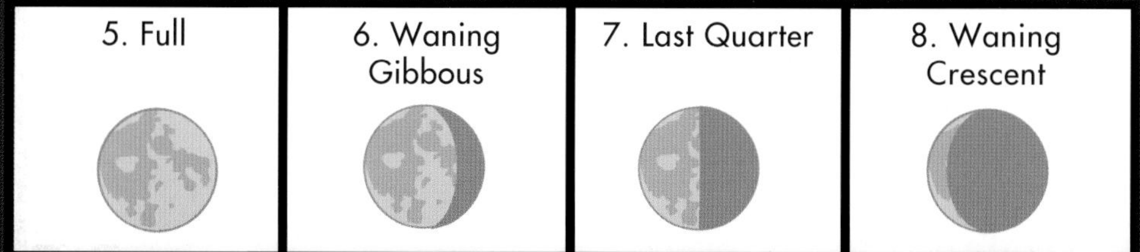

5. Full	6. Waning Gibbous	7. Last Quarter	8. Waning Crescent

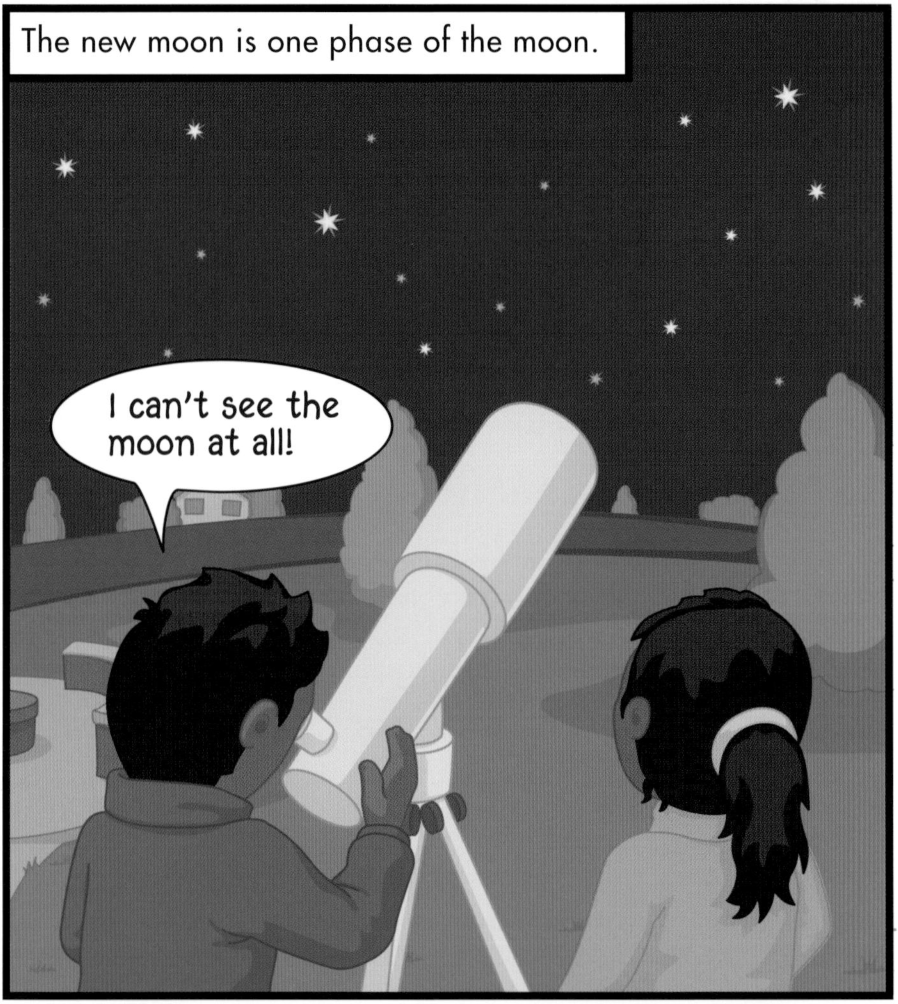
The new moon is one phase of the moon.
I can't see the moon at all!

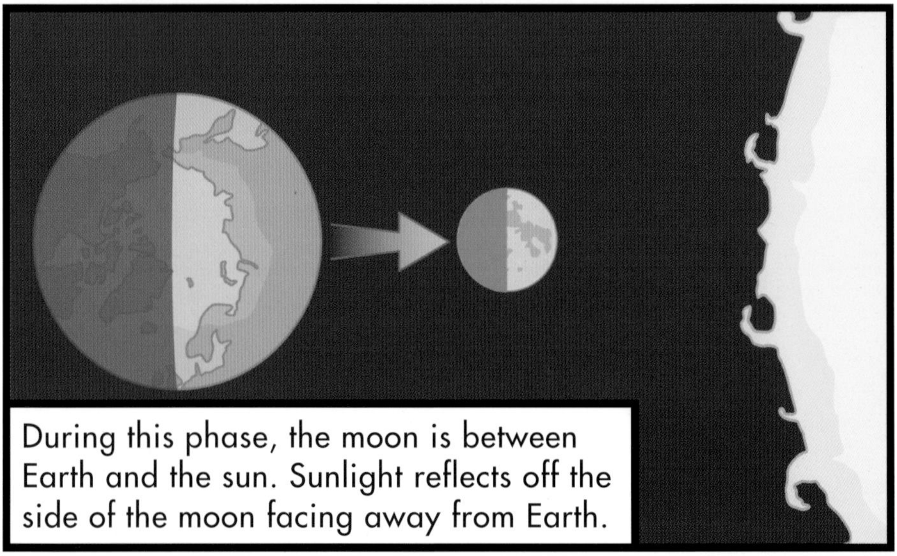
During this phase, the moon is between Earth and the sun. Sunlight reflects off the side of the moon facing away from Earth.

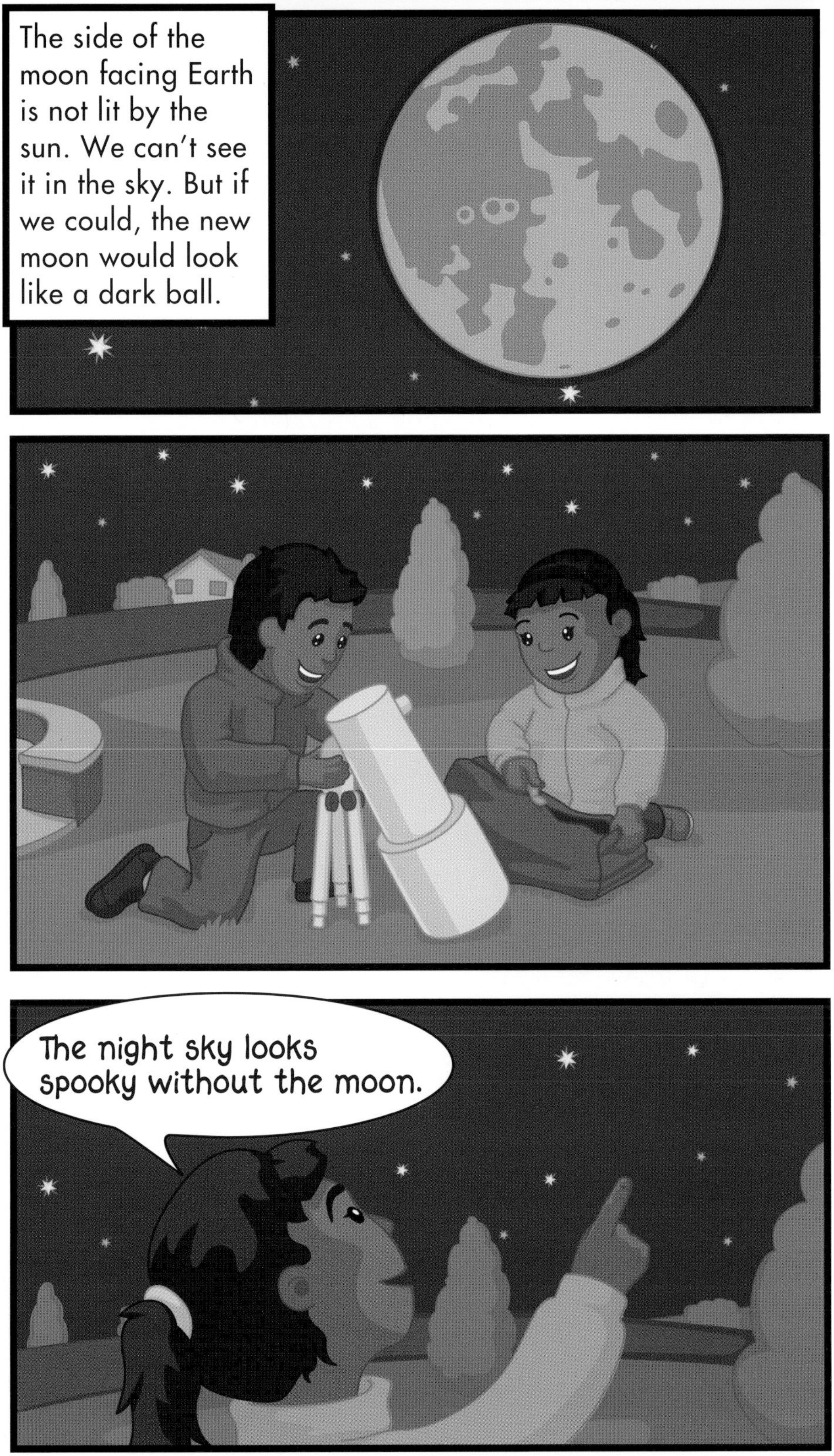
The side of the moon facing Earth is not lit by the sun. We can't see it in the sky. But if we could, the new moon would look like a dark ball.
The night sky looks spooky without the moon.

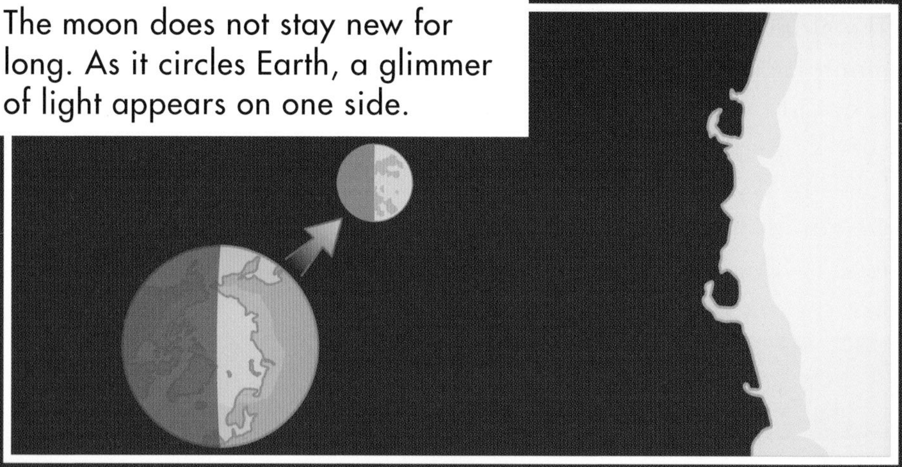
The moon does not stay new for long. As it circles Earth, a glimmer of light appears on one side.

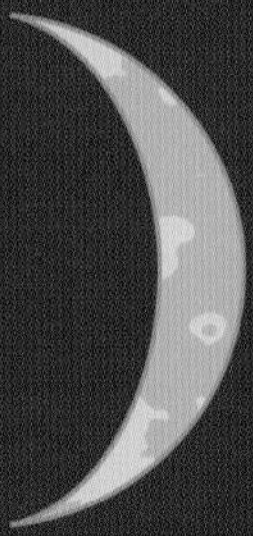
We see part of the moon reflecting sunlight. After a few nights, the glimmer grows into a crescent shape.

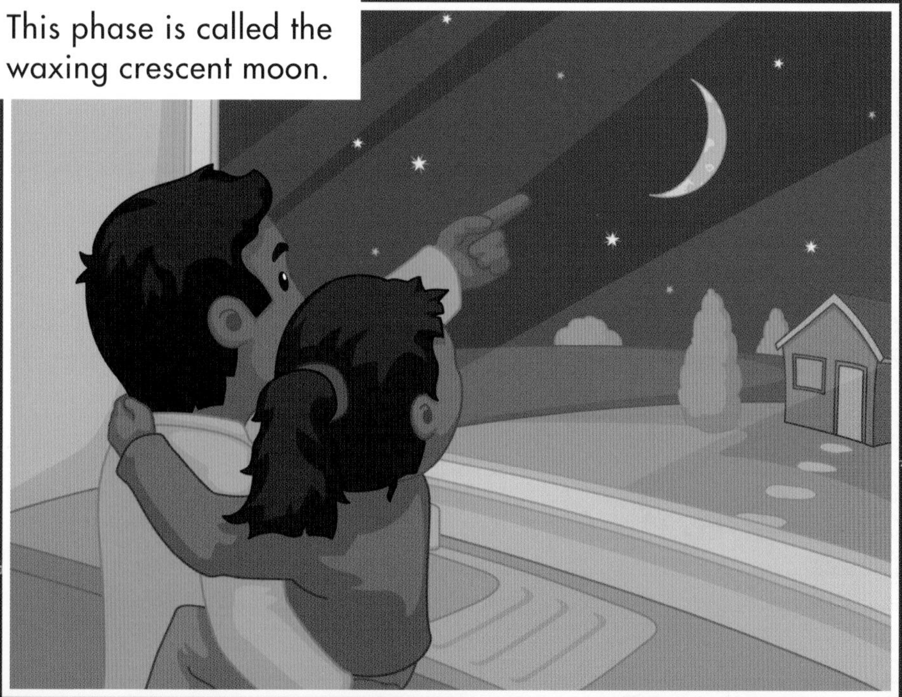
This phase is called the waxing crescent moon.

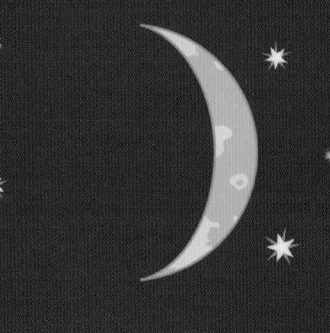

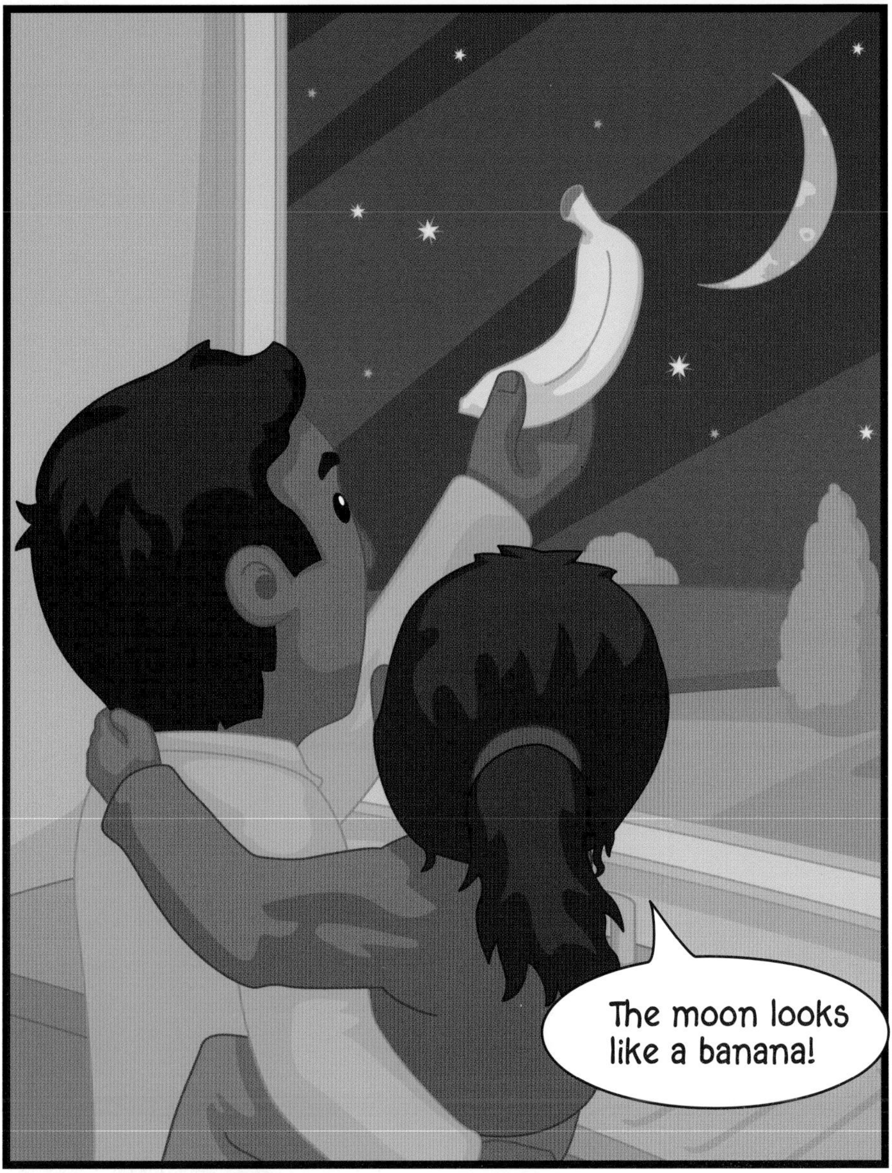
The moon looks like a banana!

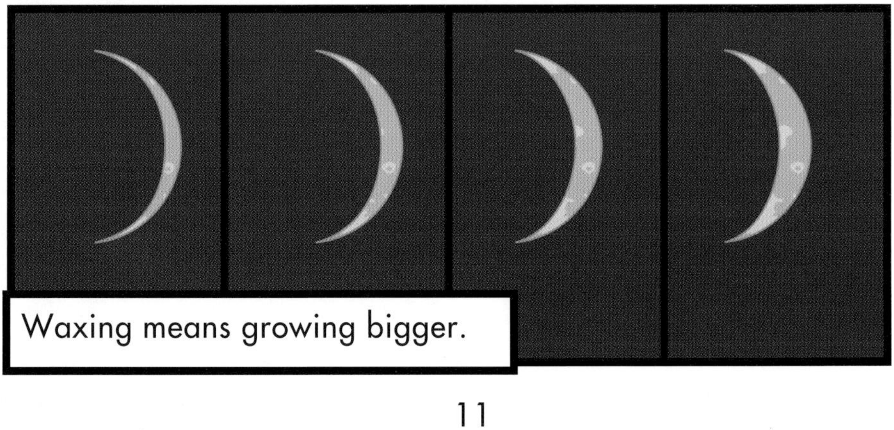
Waxing means growing bigger.

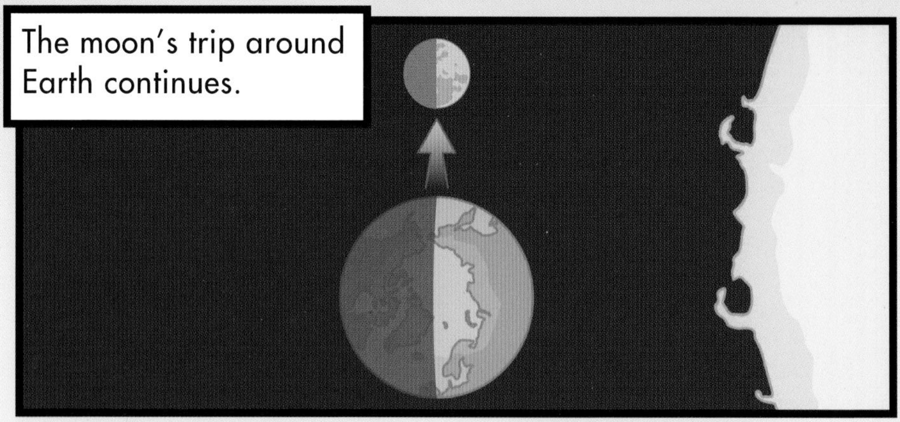
The moon's trip around Earth continues.

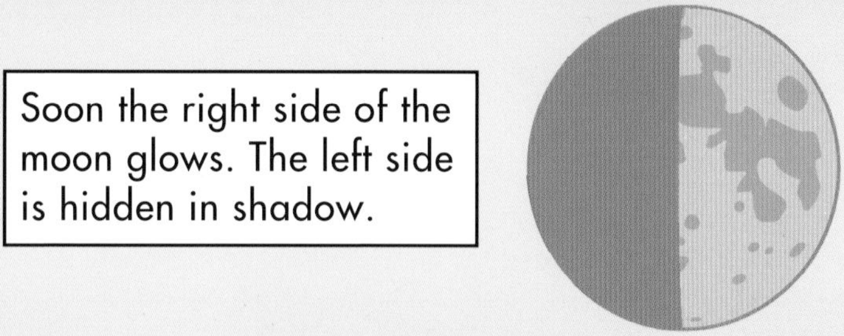
Soon the right side of the moon glows. The left side is hidden in shadow.

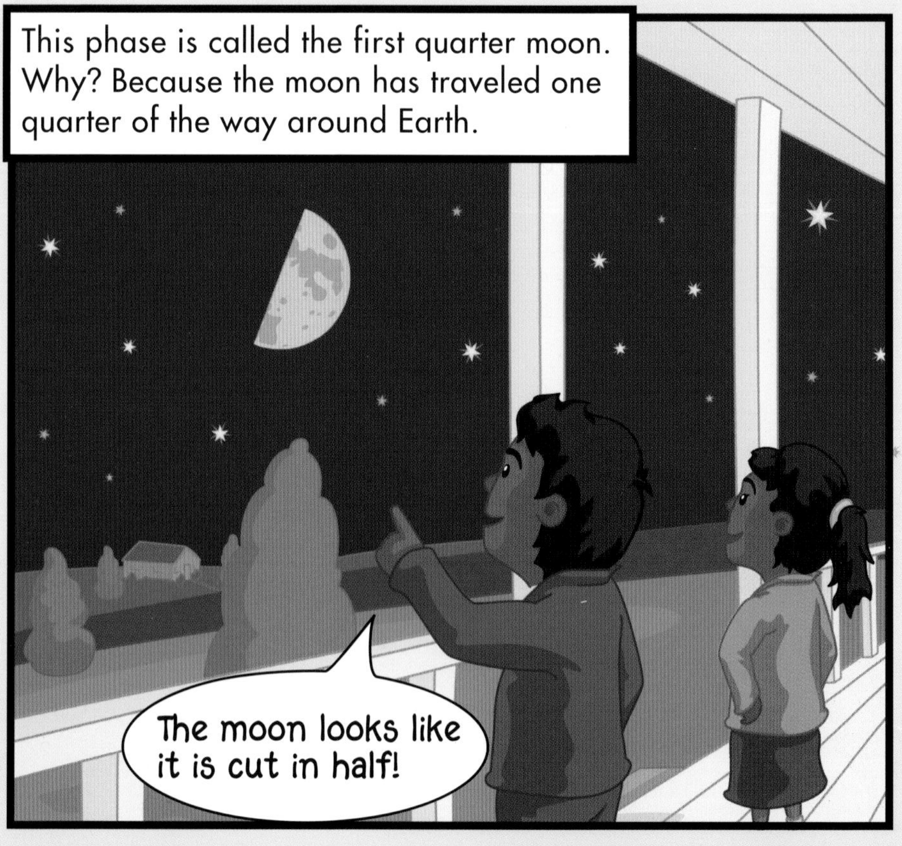
This phase is called the first quarter moon. Why? Because the moon has traveled one quarter of the way around Earth.
The moon looks like it is cut in half!

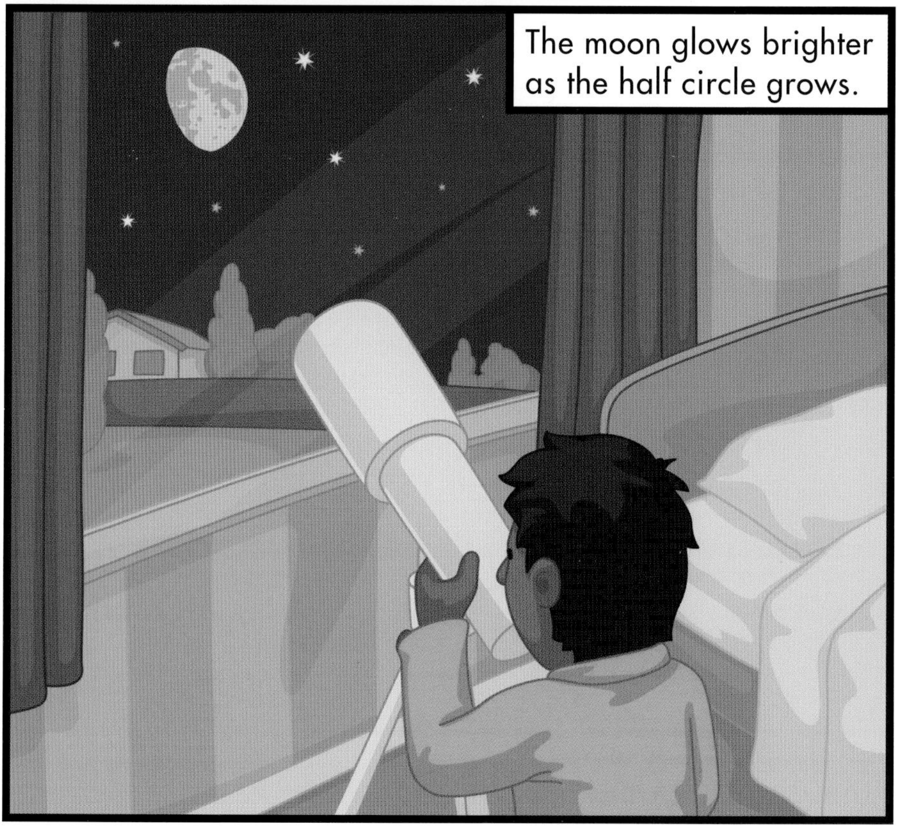
The moon glows brighter as the half circle grows.

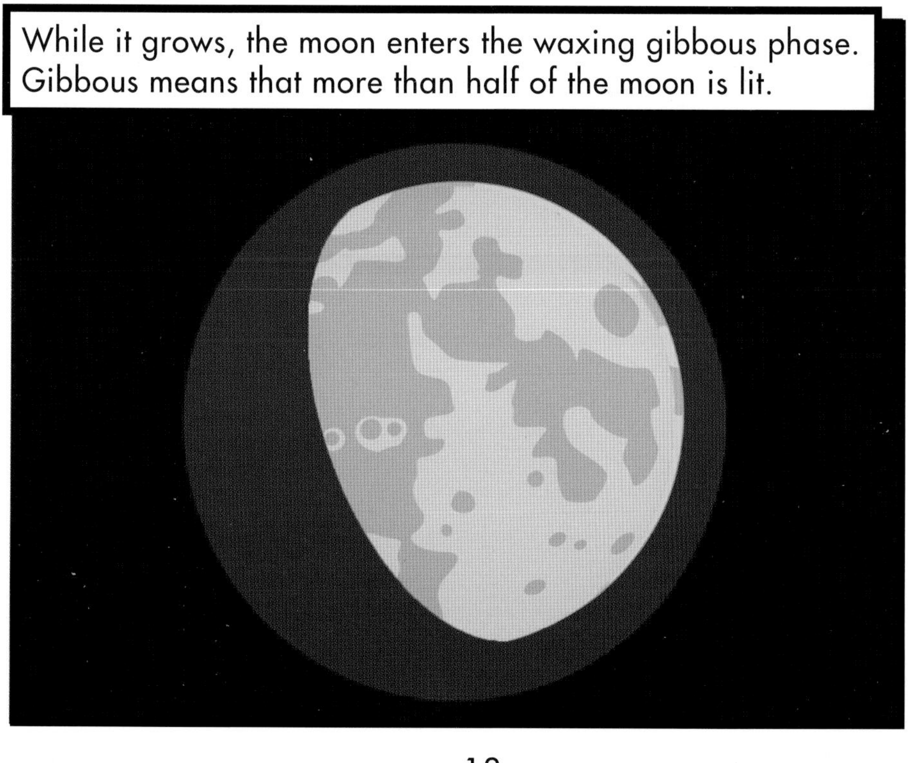
While it grows, the moon enters the waxing gibbous phase. Gibbous means that more than half of the moon is lit.

Pie in the Sky!

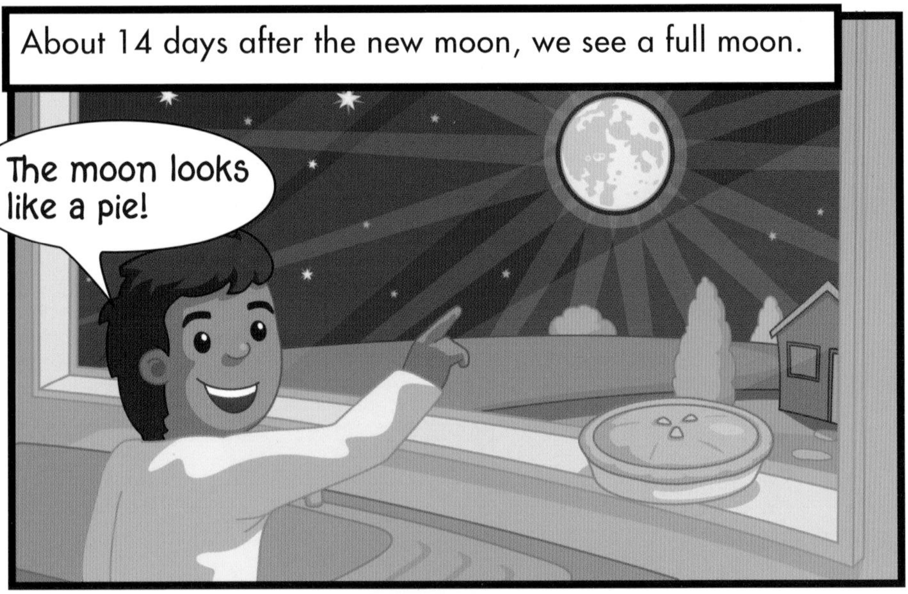
About 14 days after the new moon, we see a full moon.
The moon looks like a pie!

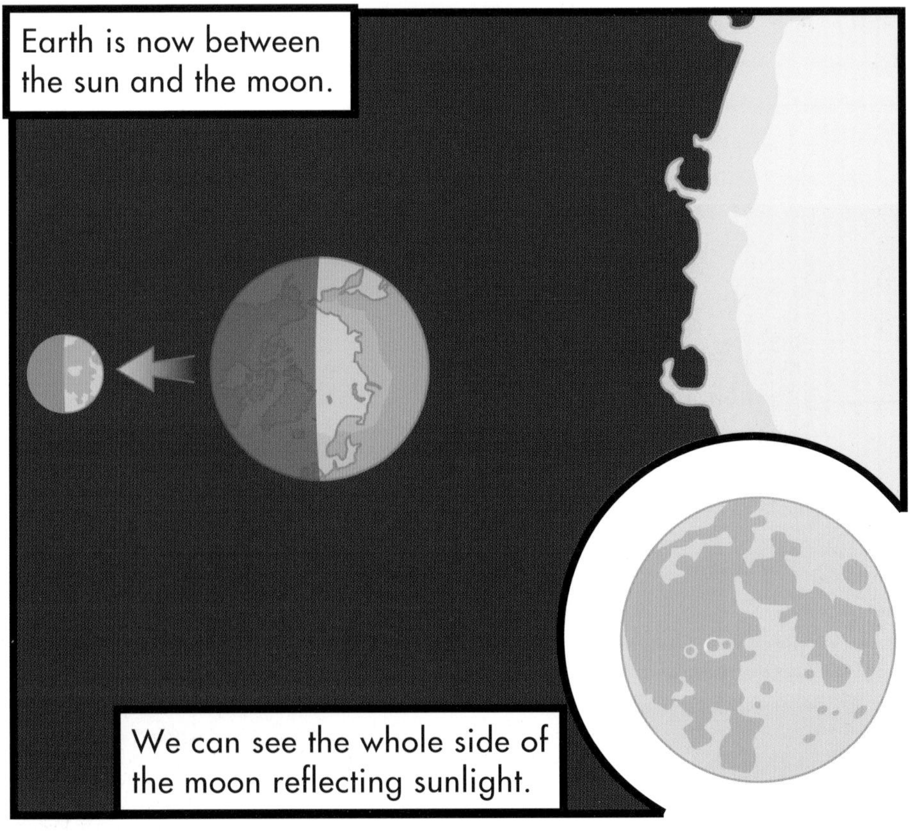
Earth is now between the sun and the moon.
We can see the whole side of the moon reflecting sunlight.

On a cloudless night, the glow from a full moon lights up the land. The reflected light casts shadows in the night.

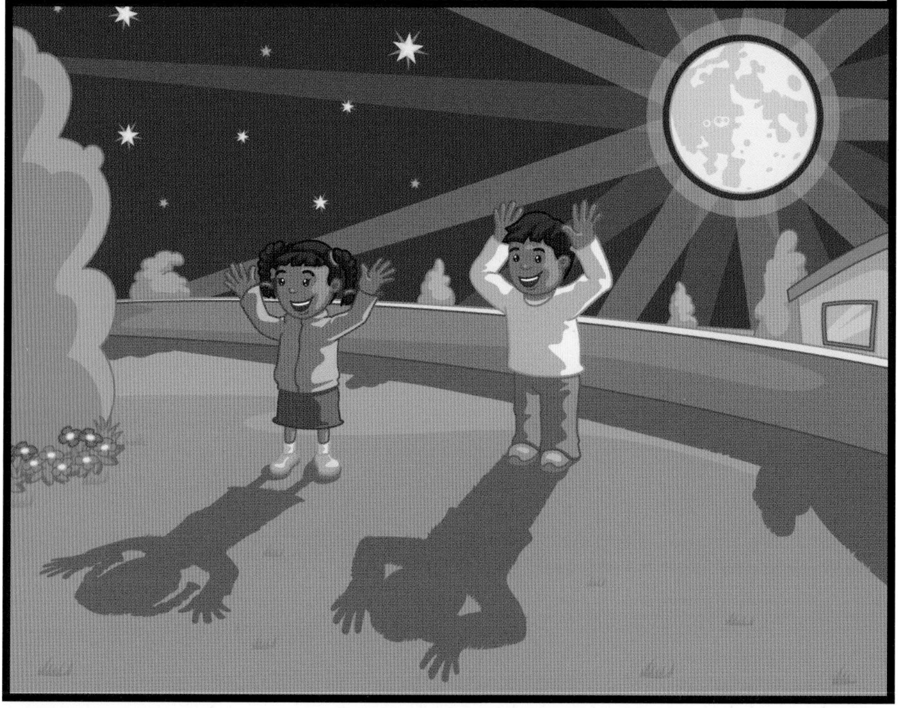

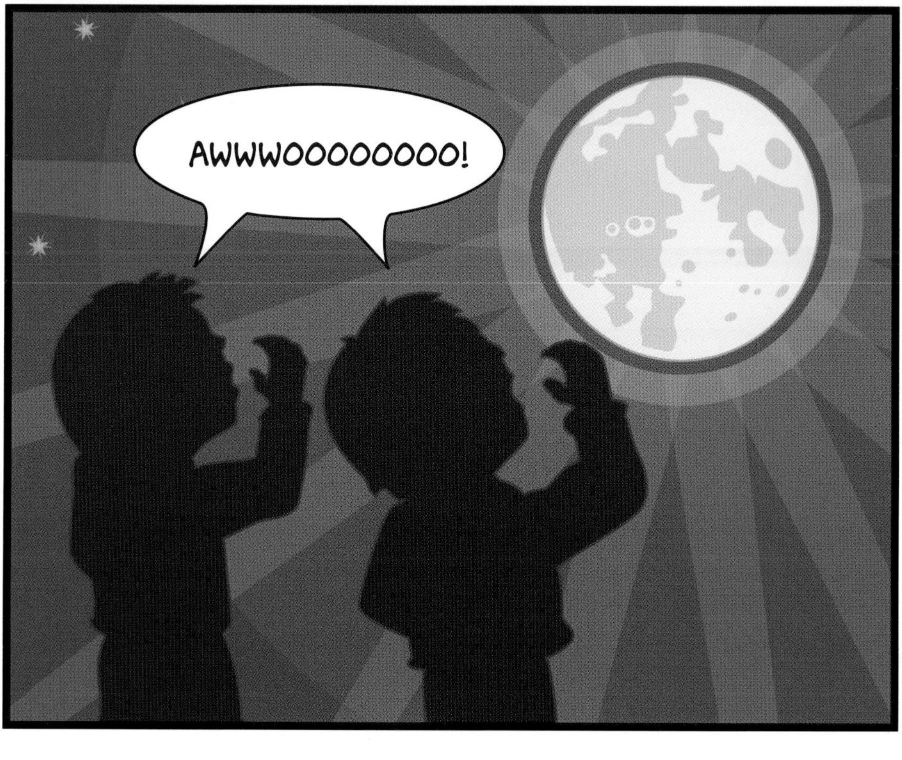
AWWWOOOOOOOO!

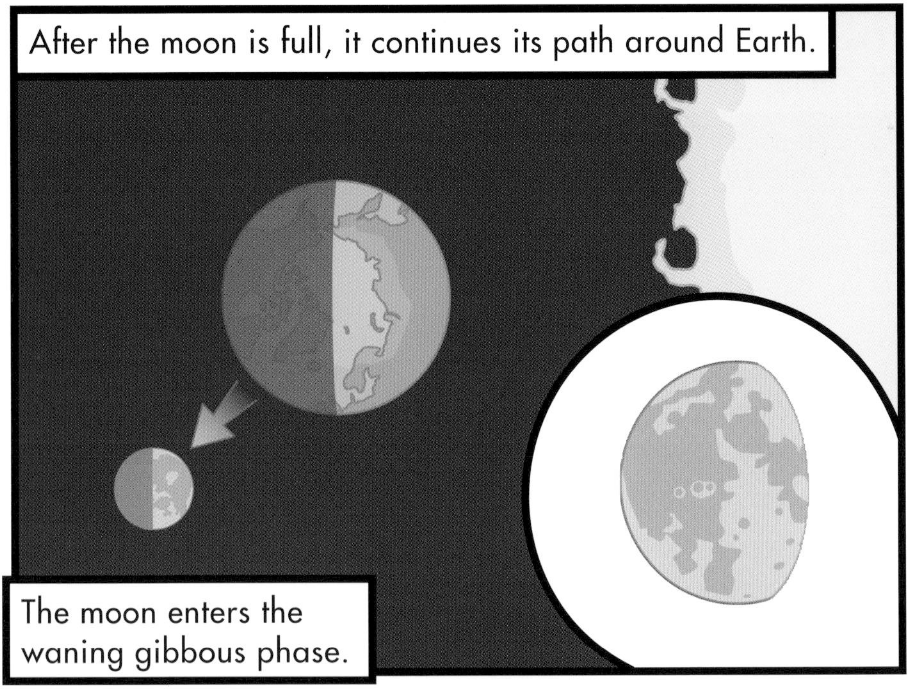
After the moon is full, it continues its path around Earth.
The moon enters the waning gibbous phase.

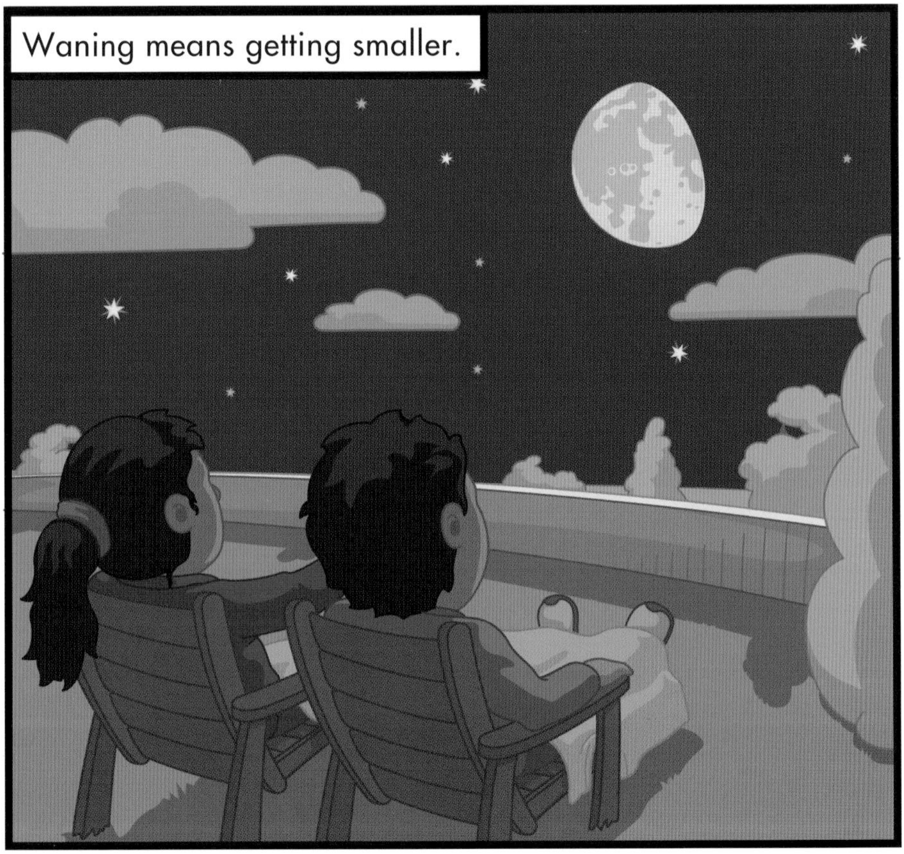
Waning means getting smaller.

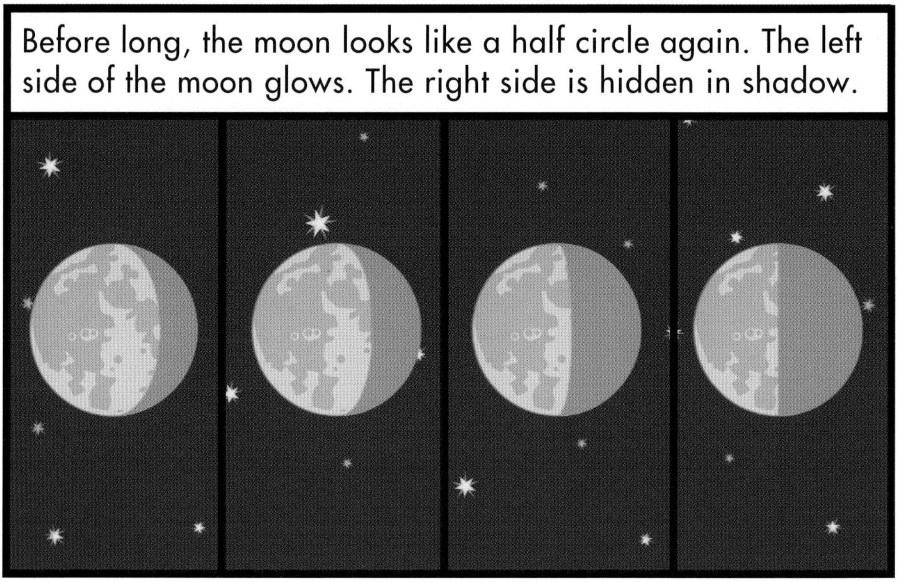
Before long, the moon looks like a half circle again. The left side of the moon glows. The right side is hidden in shadow.

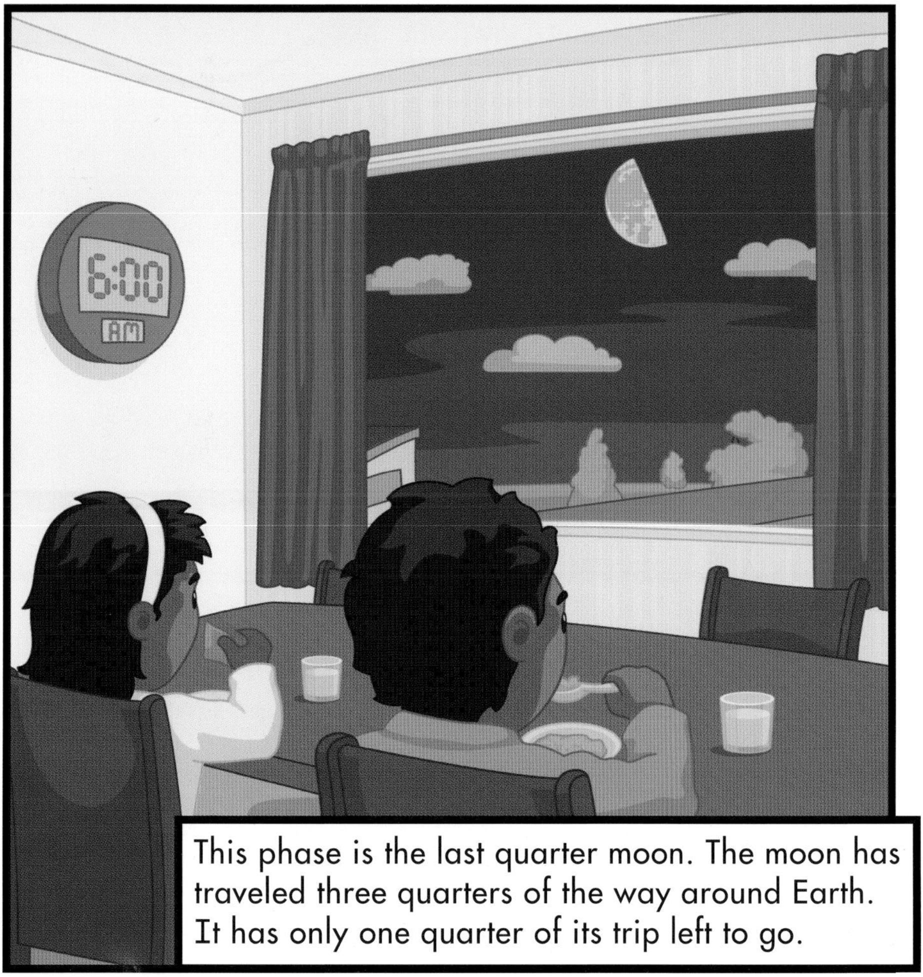
6:00
AM
This phase is the last quarter moon. The moon has traveled three quarters of the way around Earth. It has only one quarter of its trip left to go.

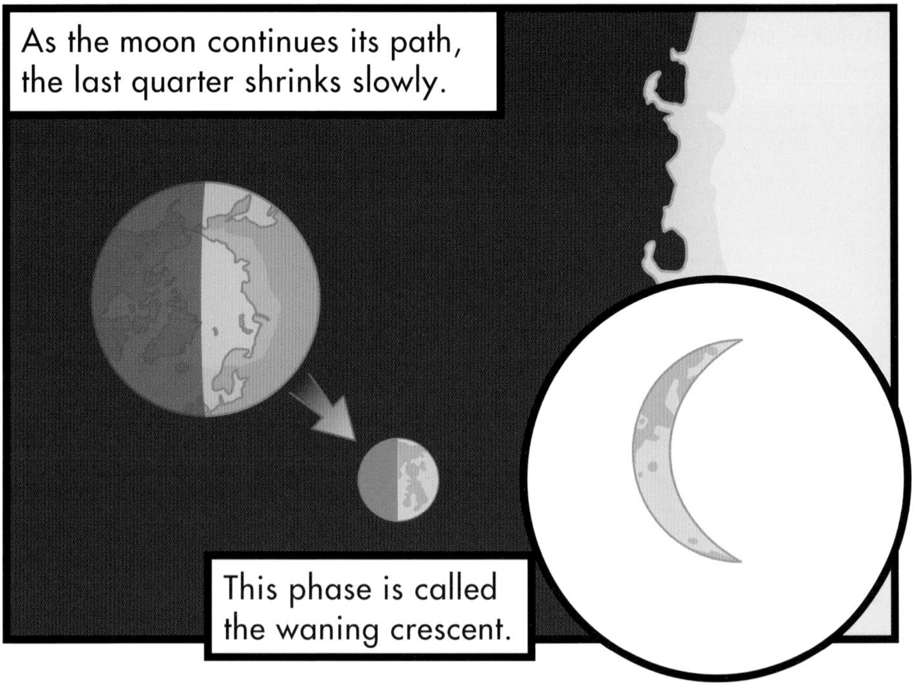
As the moon continues its path, the last quarter shrinks slowly.
This phase is called the waning crescent.

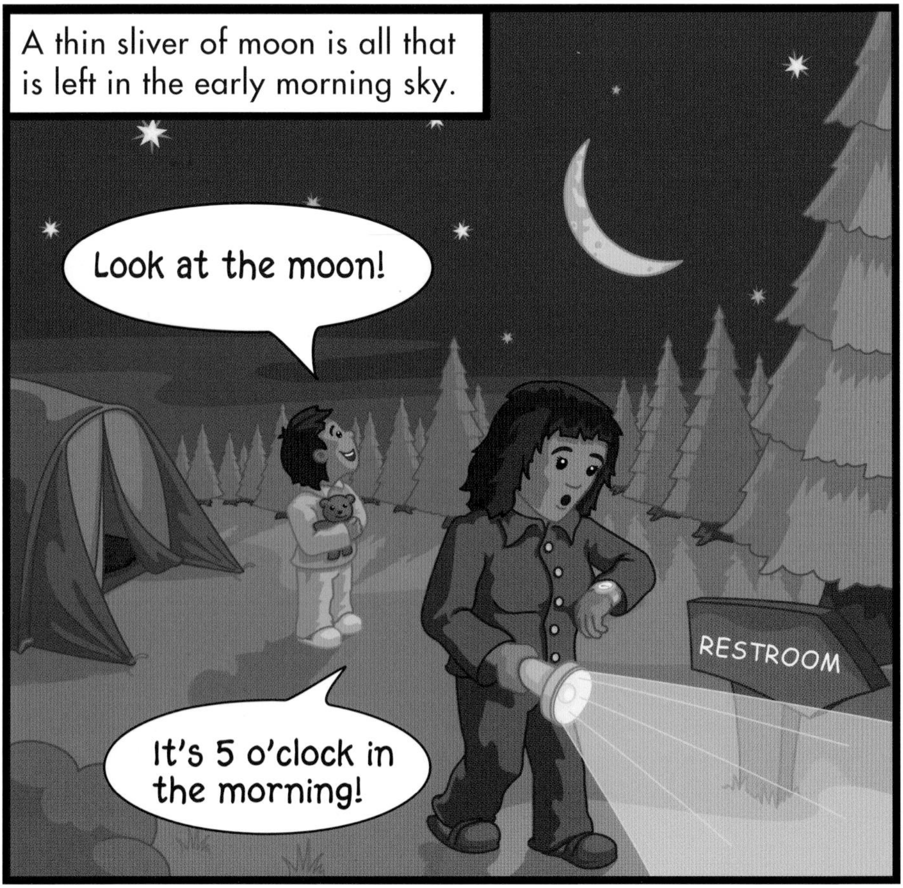
A thin sliver of moon is all that is left in the early morning sky.
Look at the moon!
RESTROOM
It's 5 o'clock in the morning!

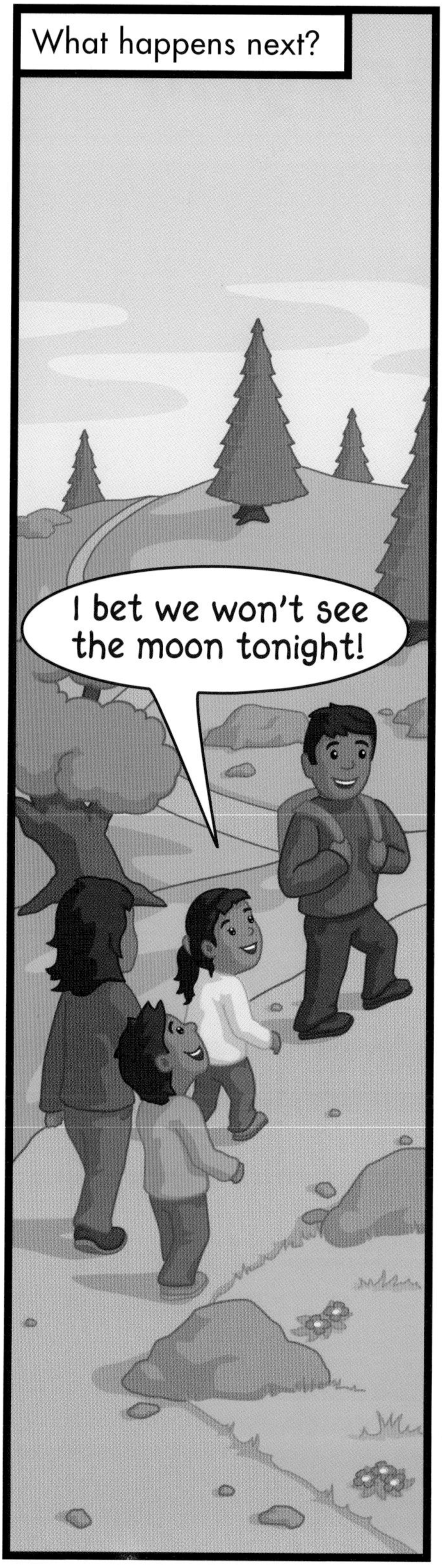
What happens next?
I bet we won't see the moon tonight!

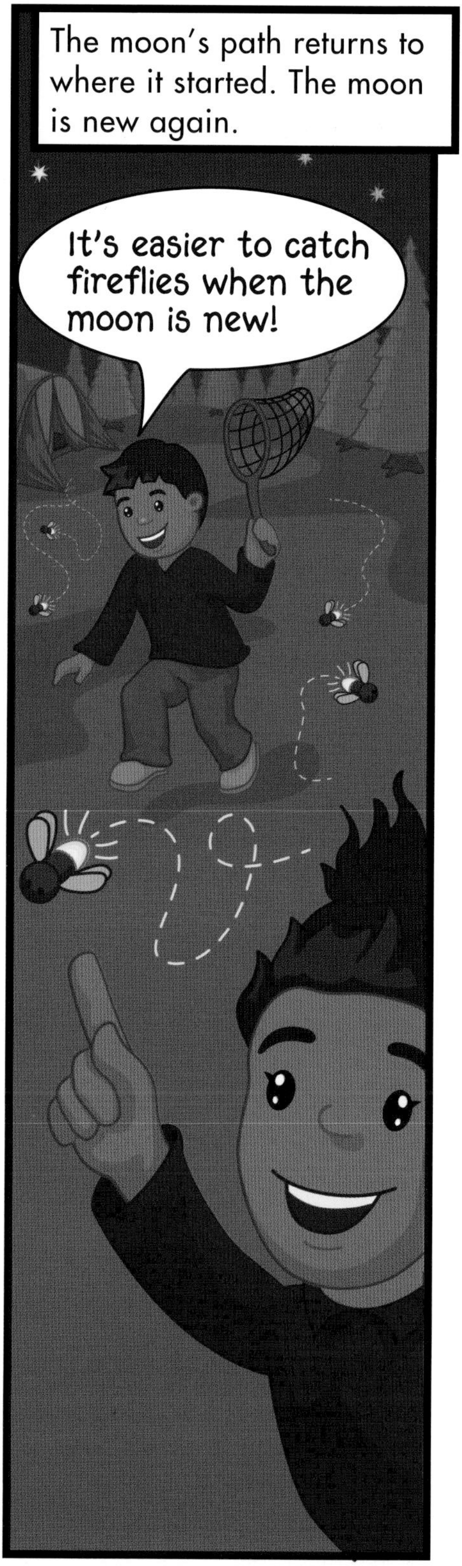
The moon's path returns to where it started. The moon is new again.
It's easier to catch fireflies when the moon is new!

Starting Over Again

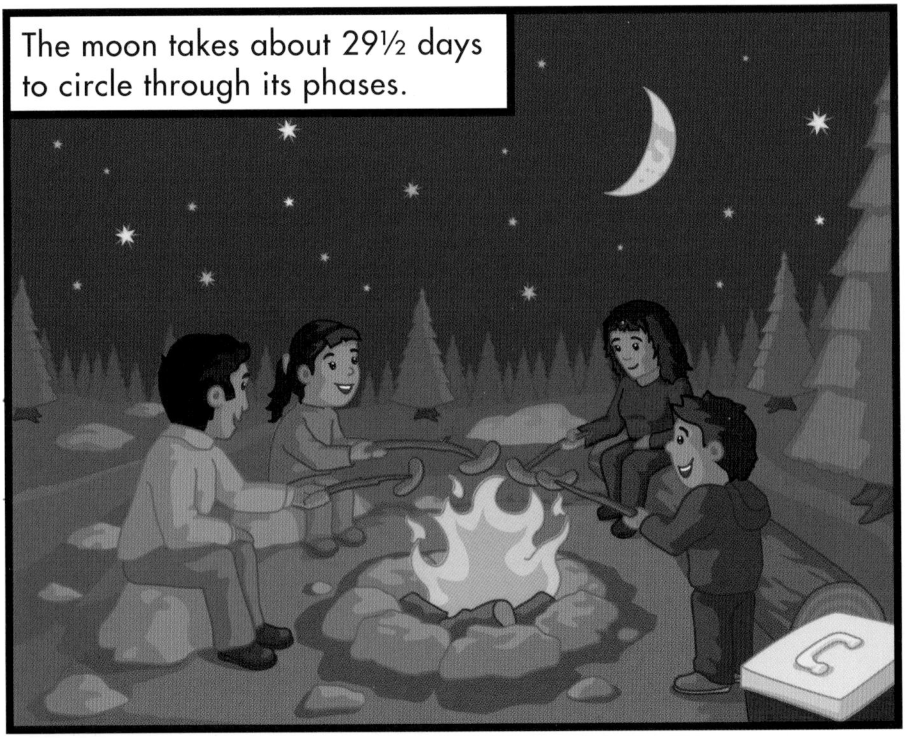
The moon takes about 29½ days to circle through its phases.

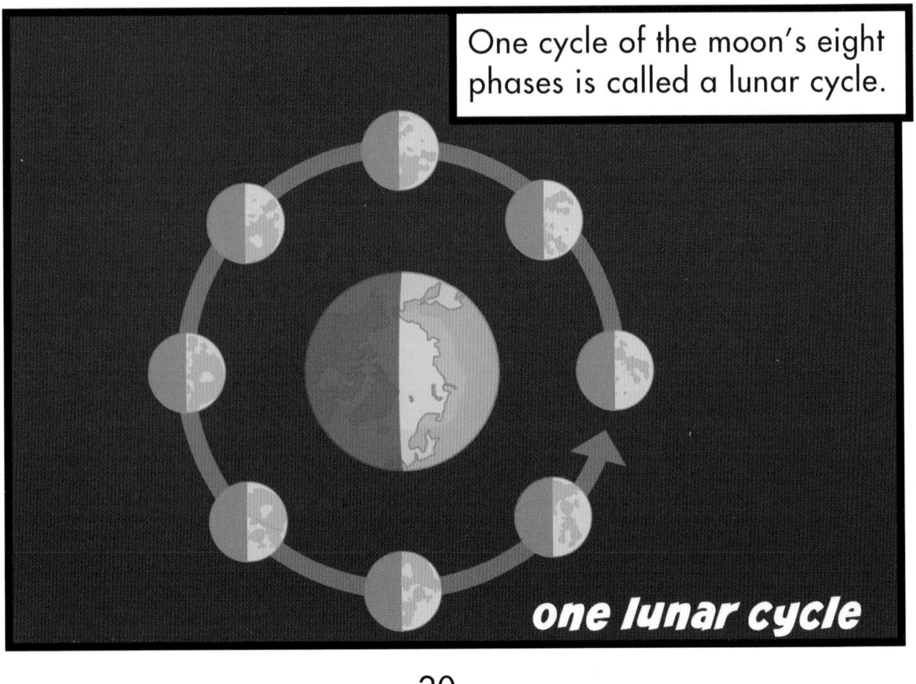
One cycle of the moon's eight phases is called a lunar cycle.
one lunar cycle

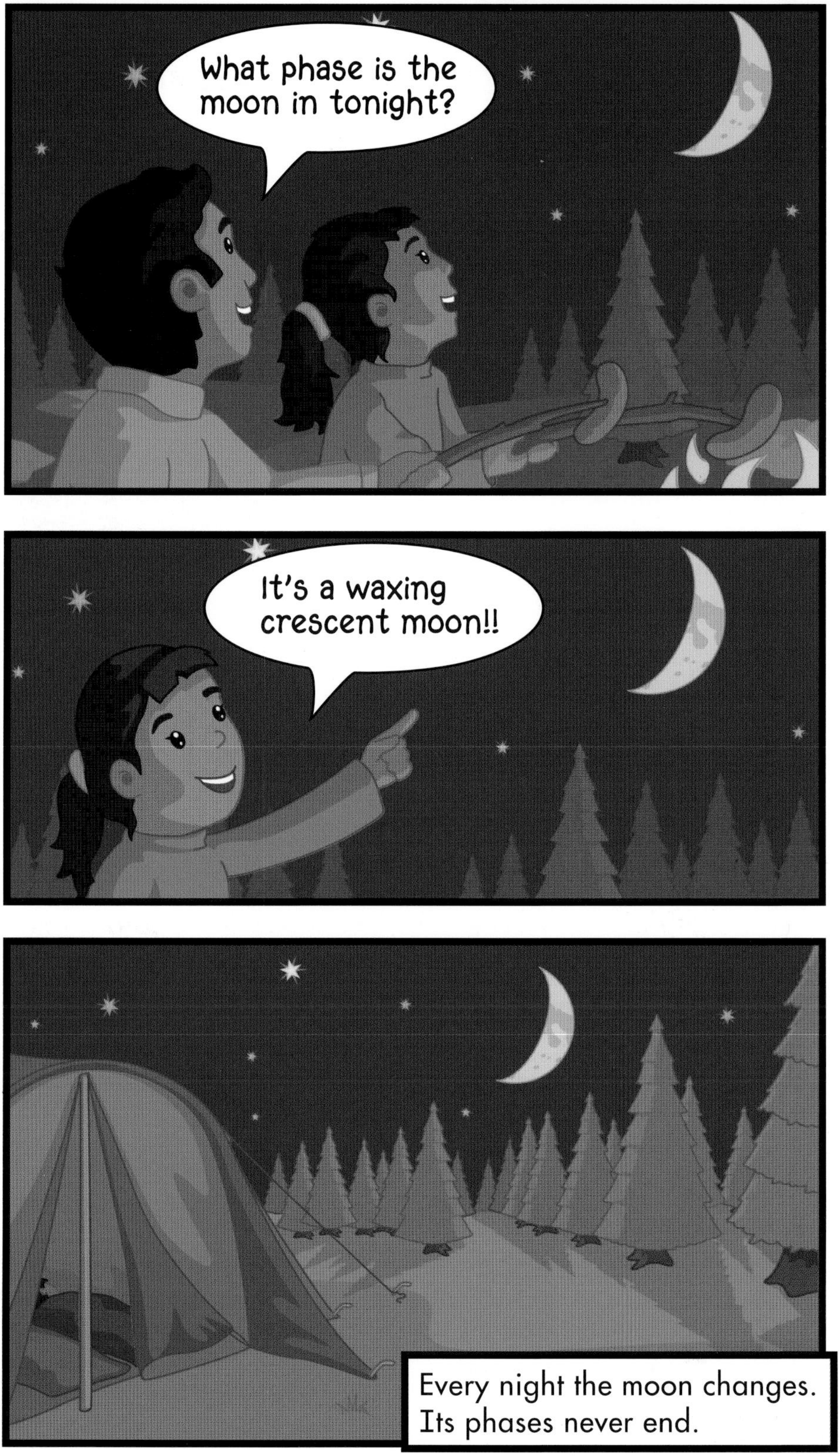
What phase is the moon in tonight?
It's a waxing crescent moon!!
Every night the moon changes. Its phases never end.

Glossary

crescent—a curved shape

cycle—something that happens over and over again

gibbous—a moon that is more than half lit

lunar—having to do with the moon

phase—a stage; the moon's phases are the shapes that it appears to take over 29½ days

reflect—to bounce back light

quarter—one of four equal parts

wane—to become smaller in size

wax—to become larger in size

Read More

Crelin, Bob. *Faces of the Moon.* Watertown, Mass.: Charlesbridge, 2009.

Olson, Gillia. *Phases of the Moon.* Patterns in Nature. Mankato, Minn.: Capstone Press, 2007.

Stewart, Melissa. *Why Does the Moon Change Shape?* Tell Me Why, Tell Me How. New York: Marshall Cavendish Benchmark, 2009.

Internet Sites

FactHound offers a safe, fun way to find Internet sites related to this book. All of the sites on FactHound have been researched by our staff.

Here's all you do:

Visit *www.facthound.com*

Type in this code: 9781429653657

Check out projects, games and lots more at
www.capstonekids.com

Index

TITLES IN THIS SET:

EGGS, LEGS, WINGS
A Butterfly Life Cycle

HIDE and SEEK MOON
The Moon Phases

SEED, SPROUT, FRUIT
An Apple Tree Life Cycle

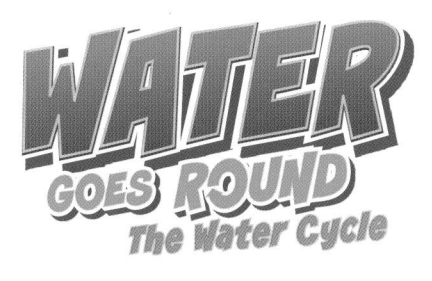

WATER GOES ROUND
The Water Cycle